MOJAVE GHOST
A Novel Poem

MOJAVE GHOST

A Novel Poem

Forrest Gander

A NEW DIRECTIONS PAPERBOOK ORIGINAL

Manufactured in the United States of America
First published as New Directions Paperbook 1614 in 2024.

Library of Congress Control Number: 2024032087

2 4 6 8 10 9 7 5 3 1

New Directions Books are published for James Laughlin
by New Directions Publishing Corporation
80 Eighth Avenue, New York 10011

"Isn't it often in our most intimate relations that we come to realize that our identity, all identity, is combinatory?"

—from *Twice Alive*

AUTHOR'S NOTE

The first dirt I tasted was a fistful of siltstone dust outside the house where I was born in the Mojave Desert. My father wasn't around much. When she could, my mother took long walks around the multicolored washes and canyons of Barstow's Rainbow Basin, now designated a National Natural Landmark. Her accounts of the changing light on the rock walls, of her encounters with silence and sidewinders, and her accumulating collection of fossils— including a broken camel rib and a piece of mastodon tooth plucked from sedimentary formations after rain— piqued my enthusiasm for earth science and led me to earn a degree in geology, the profession, it has been said, of those given to disinter memory. I became obsessed with deserts and went on to explore others: the Gobi, the Sahara, the Atacama, the Thar, the Chihuahua, and more. My mother died during the pandemic in 2021, but whenever I return to the Mojave Desert, I truly, not metaphorically, feel her ghost in the ever-so-light breeze. I see the landscape through her voice, her eyes.

Five years after the death of my wife, the poet C.D. Wright, and just two years after my mother's death, I began to walk sections of the 800-mile San Andreas Fault, from north to south. I was accompanied by a new immigrant to the country, Ashwini Bhat. Eventually, the two of us found ourselves in the Mojave, in that desolate town where I was born. As my memories and the present mixed, as my tumultuous inner emotions and the landscape coalesced, I felt my sense of self become kaleidoscopic. History, a geologist knows, is never far below the surface. Along the desert's and my own fault lines, I found myself crossing permeable dimensions of time and space, correlating my emotions and the stricken landscape with other divisions, the fractures and folds that underlie not only my country, but any self in its relationship with others.

MOJAVE GHOST

Men arm themselves with facts.
They say, already reaching, Let me
see that. They ask, seriously, Who
is your second favorite tenor sax player
between '63 and '65? Each
thinks the other is a bit emptier, more
cardboard than himself, that he alone
made the necessary decisions. Only
I live the real real, he thinks. I think.

Night wind clanging rope against the flagpole.

There is nothing in me now
of what I was before. That's
what he tells himself. In order
to live with himself.

Nearly midnight. On the dimly moonlit
porch, his boots lined up neatly
at the front door. Three of the four
black laces are tucked into the boots' collars
but one has gone loose, spilling from the eyelet
to the concrete like a thin blood trail.

I found my necessity, too, was provisional,
and whatever was essential in me had gone slack
behind certain irrevocable choices I made.

She asked quietly if he noticed.
What? *How the small moths come out*
at dusk, but the big ones— these, she said
casting her eyes into the darkness,
only after midnight.

A studied lack of correlation between his eyes,
intent on her lips, and what he wants, which is
somewhere else.

That spangled negation she so casually calls *evening*.

It all changes
in the seconds it takes for a parasite
in the saliva of a sand fly
to replicate itself in the gut
and migrate to the fly's proboscis.

Waking alone
into the faintly semen-smell of the middle of the night.

*

Back here, he imagines her
everywhere he looks. As the spring hills boing green.

All awake are the crows.

Flayed by the paper cut of her scent in his memory.

For her, it was home. This town
where various stirps of Christian
fundamentalism intersect
with unchecked retail sprawl.

Now the train just pass on through.

One man hosing out a cement mixer
at the gravel pit. A form of forced confession.

Bright afternoon, and the young woman walks slowly
to her car across the Mastectomy Center parking lot.

How our friend died here: disheveled, looking
down and reading a book as he hiked
along the shoulder of the interstate.

However long I mean to hold on to them
as possibilities, my untaken trajectories begin
to shrivel away from my self-identification.

What he remembers is her voice charged
with enthusiasms. And that point of inflection
in his life when he saw she knew how he was
awed by her disciplined inattention. *Oh,*
she had added, ecstatic, *and I love
the smell of breeder houses after rain.*

*

Back at Lana's Diner, watching the woman
at the far table sweep her hair to her other shoulder
and flash her teeth at her companion.

Red sauce, says the woman when her eggs come,
and the waitress returns with ketchup.

As I'm picking up my check
from the table where I've eaten alone,
the waitress calls *Come again*, and
instinctively I answer, *We will.*

Handwritten note near the cash register:
Do Not Lean Arm on Pecan Roll.

So I pay up and step into humid
rock-flavored afternoon heat.
Dark pompadour clouds casting giant shadows.

Gonna be a gully-washer.

Technically it is stunned, not
dead. And though the retractable bolt
has obliterated the cow's brain,
the nicotine Saturn of its still-
open eye seems to regard me.

What bird wove those sprigs of lavender, mint, yarrow,
and citronella into a nest below our rusted porch light?

Just before the rain begins to blow more rain against the rain.

*

Wiper blades splashing me as
the gas station attendant hands me my change.

When our friend's divorce was finalized and
I helped her move to an apartment, she turned
and asked me where I thought
she should place the placenta jar.

Out of friendship. Out of whatever
my services make of friendship.

What is it you're thinking, your forehead knotted up like that?
I was thinking of you.
What were you thinking?

From the rain-blurred window of the notions shop
where you liked to go, a kneeling Elamite bull-god,
carved from alabaster, holds out a ritual vessel
to the torrential oncoming, a world forever in motion.

He must have watched you too pass by.

I'm staring at a photo of myself as a child.
Who IS that person now? Some infant
with receding gums, a widow's
peak, and hair swirling inside his ears.
Proof of an unendurable afterwards.

I just want it to be real, you said.

But no matter how I tried,
I couldn't shake the unreal out of me.

A single coyote howling from Eden Isle.

*

Because he was angry
or because he was depressed and denied it
or because he loathed, was laded with self-loathing,
because he soaked in disappointment and boorishness, because
depression swallows sound as mud swallows
rain, the finer pleas and raw cries of pain
he was eliciting from those he loved didn't reach him.

Now, he finds there's no way
to mind the gap between first- and third-
person perspectives. His

perception of the world
oscillates in and out
of referential focus. I simply
finds no way.

Like trying to straddle the scuttle in the attic.

Nor between the publicity of the world
and the self's interiority.

Nor, for that matter, between past and present.

For still, I pre-assume you before I catch myself
staring into space, wanting to tell you something.

Much of my experience is indistinct. (*God
help me*, I think, vaguely). But
every moment rivets you into me.

*

Orange lichen on the broken-tile roof of the church—
Raucous grackles shifting in the twilight oaks of the square—
The sun's last ray strikes the bell-gable—
And the old Spanish-speaking man
studying me from the church steps
touches his index finger below his right eye,
pulls the flesh down from his lower lid,
and afflicts me with arthritis.

My branches bend toward the ground now.

There is no joy in looking back at joy.
Says the hardened arterial self.

Lower your damper, youngblood.

But which self blinks back like a newt
from the bathroom mirror?

She had aimed at him the undiminished
beam of her love with all her mind and
heart and soul, but the whole while
he was thinking of something else, he was
someplace else. Unaccountable.

And feeling rushes in now, a little
late, and with it the memory of that
hammer-stunned beast
listing hard against the rail
as its brain shut down.

*

Now he's watching scarves of cloud
slide over the plane's steel wing.

Surely it's real, this swirl of light.
But the visions that confront him do not enter his life.

I borrowed my brightness from her. Where is it now?

Memento mori. And just so,
these clouds like lines of coke,
these fine bird-bone clouds
giving structure to the afternoon sky
will decompose into faint nothings.

Down below, that's not a landfill;
it's a mirror.

I don't remember having left the earth. And
yet I must have, for I don't recognize this
place or myself. It's as if I entered a strange
forest filled with warblers, and though I suspect
they're singing, my ears are bunged with tar.

Like a towering wall, higher
and higher, of meaningless words.

If language is just another kind of coordination—

if upwelling verb tenses
could draw together past and present
into an emotional harmonic—

Which is about when Langston Hughes
rhymed "feet" with "alreet."

When we find our lives
disagreeable to look at, we say
I am not *that* any longer.
I am otherwise now. Back in tune
with what I should have been.

But what bird has woven sprigs of lavender, mint, yarrow,
and citronella into a nest below our rusted porch light?

I keep revisiting the memory
of that inward flare of exhilaration
when I knew for sure what counted. But
who is ever content with contentment?

*

Though no one called, I look back again.

Searching for their night roost, tiny
birds drop like stars into the darkened dead
trees around me. I had thought

dreams were like water, that we
can't smell anything there. And then you
visited me, your body whole again
but with the must of extinction on your breath.

*

The coffee capsule still lodged in the machine,
the used cup precarious near the edge
of a bureau across from the bed
with its white tumble of duvet
and sheets. Just a sprinkle of urine
on the toilet seat and the closet agape
as I close the door on another unremarkable
hotel room in a place charged with memories
I cannot metabolize.

Maybe Pascal had it wrong. It's not
that our problems stem from an inability
to sit quietly in a room alone,
but that our problems, so
precisely coincident with us,
suck up all the room's air,
leaving us no choice but to flee
or be expunged.

Two caged hounds alert and focused intently
on the front porch door. Early morning. Smoke
from the chimney.

Down at Lake Echo, shrink-wrapped
boats, like huge cocoons, make ready
to sleep off the winter.

It's not that I is another, but that my life is always elsewhere.

*By the third round he really hit
his poses, but he'd already lost his pump.*

When morning brightens, you step outside
in your Leonard Cohen shirt to find
the yard carpeted with Monarch butterflies
killed off by early frost.

The barge is back today, propped on one steel leg
at the stern and two at the bow, digging up
clay and gravel from the lake bottom. A woman,
working two pedals with her feet and two joysticks
with her hands, guides its clamshell bucket filled
with muck, while black wads of smoke pour out
from muffler canisters that cap the exhaust tubing.

Immediately I jog home,
knowing how much you'll want to see this.

As I pull you along, you tell me
Loki piloted an assault ship fashioned
from the fingernails of the dead.

And the lake's small waves
go on wringing themselves out in the sand.

After years of amputations, the sycamore limbs
by the courthouse end in huge, mangled fists.

In memory, the upside-down
reflection of you
approaching from behind
crawls up the stainless steel hood
of the water fountain's spout
toward my mouth.

Is it odd that what we remember
is confined so often to particular moments
like still images ripped from a film?

Rummaging through the bin ends.

A new voicing for each chorus
arranged so that the sequence
supports the building tension.

It's hard to make that curly sound.

A dozen grouse strung up
in the barbershop window
with a wire through their nostrils.

He examines an infinite horizon
he cannot approach.

Dressed to the nines for New Year's, they stand together
a moment before the mirror. Does she catch
a trace of cowardice lodged in the corners of his eyes?

I feel such sympathy, she says, for those who never learn
to use time unprofitably.

And those who believe that birds chatter idly? For them,
the journey is over. Their luck has already flickered out.

As hundreds of sandhill cranes take flight over Lodi, honking
en masse, circling. Then they drain away into a darkening sky.

*

But how do you tell which of the tree rings is false?

As though there's a sound I'm trying to make
that I can only imagine by its difference
from the sounds my mouth is making now,
from all the sounds I've made. And yet it's
there, I can recall it as feeling and as metaphor,
just under my tongue, a name
drawn in the dirt and stamped out,
a caress drafting in a tailwind. Mute
but stirring, like an anthill in the morning sun.

In molecular sand at the base of the cliff,
pale fossils appear after the rain, mostly
ammonites and bryozoa. Speaking to me.

Which is when the raft of dabbling wigeons explodes.

*

As latent with futurity as a closed stopcock,
the dawn redwood before it leafs out.
While in a brief sideshow, our lives take place nearby.

It's so contagious: your quick, rubato, navel laugh.

Walking side by side
through Armstrong Woods,
its terpinated air strong as snuff,
we feel the kick-in of elation.

Only in your company do I
concentrate and hold together
like the tightening vortex of a tornado.

Veritas sequitur esse rerum.

*

Snorting at the uselessness of poetry, the proctologist
we meet at the New Year's party is armed
with a restricted vocabulary of catch phrases and
pomposities. A mind, you whisper to me
as we turn away, can rivel up like an old apple.

The words become so small, they cannot stand.

That anxious self of habit.

Need a light?

Not, you say, to fall back
endlessly into the routine of ourselves.
Nor to compose ourselves always
from the same syllables.

We lie listening to the ilmenite dark,
to the thrum of rain. Sleep comes
while the light goes on
waiting for us somewhere else. I

must sometimes seem to you
like a clumsy, excitable ape,
or like a Shih Tzu, excitable
and clumsy as an ape. Or like
a big baby whose face has been
transformed by magisterial wrinkles.

Everything comes to us,
but only after extraordinary exertion,
and when, finally, it comes, there
is no place to put the rest.

My childhood self asks again,
What have you done with your life?

All night from the roof, the plinking and
oscillating tympanum of the downpour.

*

Because the tree line opens contours of meanings
other than the ones for which we're prepared,
we treat it with suspicion.

When he smiled and shook his head no, his face
connoted the presumption that you and I live in a different world.
He took us in like the scent of a dead animal.

But how to sustain attentiveness? How to keep
the mind from dropping its needle
into the worn grooves of association?

My art, you said in passing, is nothing much
more than the discipline of an embodied life.

Articulating nuance. The delicate
palette. You paint details
with a tiny brush you made yourself
of hair plucked from your forearm.

They distrust me, you said, because
they can tell I prefer my work to their own.

Which is when I tucked a red anemone
under your pillow to bring you good dreams. What

else did you say?
Fair enough. It is a marriage of equals and without degree.

Your trace on me
like rope marks on the well's mouth.

Here, have a thought.

As for our misfit status: as Brecht observed,
the palace of canonical culture is built on—

Not to interpret. To feel life course through you.

*

I pour arnica into my palm and
begin to massage the tight cords
at the back of your neck.

You, who are the image-epitome of my happiness.

Only in your company do I
concentrate and hold together. Living
with you attunes me to the various
distinct moods that make me whole.
But what do I give in return?

Marriage, a divination of resonant relations.

Until right before our eyes, within minutes
of coming into contact with air, the rich
colors of the freshly excavated fresco
begin to fade to a dull grey.

Narrative, you say, is just one way of navigating time.

And those perceptions culled
by the restraints of narrative
become available to other trajectories.

Meanwhile, the future blows toward us without handholds.
It is a gaping. An already. A maw.

What happens when the mind is no longer a place of duration?

If you want to resuscitate your destiny, you joked
early in our relationship, start with the present. Which
is when, for the first time, I took in the resolute
openness of your face.

But I was a jukebox. What came out of me was just
what other people wanted to hear.

Let's let sleeping dogs tell the truth.

I see the lives of others. But not their actual lives.

The more I try to remember it, the more the word fades.

Time metamorphoses memories and buries them. There's
no restitution. Gradually, they fold in on themselves, irretrievable.

June morning. The mockingbird triggers my impulse
to respond with a standing ovation.

Because I gripped what I loved tightly, what
I've lived makes it easier for me to leave it behind
when my time comes.

Because I didn't grip tightly enough—

My younger sister died today. My
father died today. My closest friend
died today. My mother died today. Each
of their deaths detonates in iterative
simultaneity inside the tissue
of my being, unanchoring me,
setting me adrift.

Such griefs as are graves.

How is it I can continue to smolder like this? Why am I not consumed?

*

Summer roadrunners patrol the mesquite and brown
barrel cacti, snatching grasshoppers out of the air.

As you rub the sunblind from your eyes.

What to say of the pastel
chromaticism of these Mojave sunsets?

Here, as everywhere, when you go still,
what has disappeared comes forward.

Ya me cayó el veinte.

And you, an earthbound sun, a radiance.

When we return to our car parked on the laterite
verge of the road, I distract you from noticing
the dead bird melted into a gruel, its eyes
glazed with clusters of fly eggs.

Only when we reach the edges of experience
do we begin to intuit the more-than-this.

Who will contradict me if I say you were and you are?

We drive deeper into the desert, arguing
about whether it's possible
to love without reservations.

When we stop for gas in Barstow,
where I was born, a boy offers to let you hold
the horned toad he is gently stroking
in the direction of its spines.

*

Now there are creases that curve
from the flanges of my nose
to the scissure of my lips.
And a deep cleft, like something
left by a hatchet,
above the bridge of my nose.

The brusque, impersonal, obstinacy of aging.

Weeding around the bushes in front
of our house, I breathe in the slightly licorice
scent of rotting leaves.

Though it's twilight, down the street I hear
workers with their tree chipper coming nearer.

In the glimmer and darkfalling
afterglow, my small exuberances
hive in me like worms in a cadaver.

I'll just sleep for a while
with these stones over my eyes.

Don't turn away or you'll lose me.

But there you go anyway, drifting out
in the saline backwash of dream.

But doesn't thinking happen
everywhere? Not only inside
the human mind. What stays
autonomous from our concern?

You tell me a heartache is not an object of perception.
I wonder. But what do I know of your heart?

Experience is first a matter of feeling.
Even the feeling of not having a feeling.

The tokens of love we exchange
don't express love's meaning so much
as its ineffability.

So my experience of you is infinite. Never
contained within your dimensions.

2 B True

How you sit on the kitchen counter talking excitedly—
leaning forward, your elbows turned out, palms
flat on the polished granite, your fingers
buried below your posterior thighs.

It isn't through my ears I hear you.
I find myself listening with all my body.

We search out in each other's gestures
and expressions some evidence of what
goes unspoken, of what has remained
invisible inside each of us.

All this theorizing about the erotic—
an overlong introduction to no one at all.

But the wonderment that came over me at first sight of you.
I remember it in slow motion. My impetus jammed, slipped
into deep reverse. I stood there blinking like some animal
just released from hibernation.

Your intelligent gleaming voice, so often staggered with high laughter.

I was taken somewhere I haven't returned from.
Never again the same person.

Dude, you are purely titty-smacked!

Your charmingly thick calves and ankles.

Amazed. Like an insect blown by an updraft onto a mountain snowfield.

And whether we are aware or not, these years later,
the manner of our familiar, daily exchanges,
our movements, even our separate moments
of solitude are persistently relational. There's
a sub-level attunement between us. Our interactions
dilate, contract, and extend. And the feeling of all that
is the measure of how we've lived.

It's called the long encounter.

And still, the aperture hasn't narrowed.

Had I only loved before with reservations?

I married a pear tree.

Shifting light animates the room.

What is so ordinary about living every day,
as we do, at the threshold of each other?

Your emotions always visible in your eyes.

In you, I find my consequence.
My natural history.

In your company, irrelevance drains away.

But what is it that makes you special? Is it your intensity?

It's your ardor.

Never a sneeze, but a rapid parade of sneezes.

My office door opening. Smiling face peering around it.

You said you couldn't help
falling in love with me because I looked at you
with the mesmerizing gaze of a border collie.

Last night we parked in the roundabout at the end of the lane
just listening to the hiss of sodium-vapor streetlights
and watching cyclones of oak moths rising and falling.

We who are also taking place in this place.

The moon siphoned away into clouds.

Was I even there? Will I be there when you need me?

*

Before we knew of our friend's death, there
were, in the space of a few minutes,
three voice messages from other friends, each
saying, *Call me right away.*

The future blowing toward us without handholds.

What's the point of paying more attention to words
if the words are stupid?

The Salton Sea's small waves flutter
like the blank pages of a book.

*

So what if worlds are boundless? I caught
myself filling with the nonreturnable
particularity of this one afternoon. Squatting
and listening to a desert marigold bloom.
When the hum of an invisible plane
made me suddenly aware of the sprawling
underflow of stillness around me,
it was not loneliness I felt, but
some nevertheless of enchantment.

Those constant bearers of meaning
bore me. I want to open wide now
to the absence of concept, understanding,
representation, to the inward flare
of exhilaration. To the gratuitous
revelation of mineral forces. Isn't the
materiality of this Joshua tree, its living
presence, more than what it means?

*

Now the Joshua trees are withering
in the drought—"not to recover
in our lifetimes"—and the desert below them
is spalling, unstitching itself. *Now*
itself is spalling. Incrementally

making itself unavailable to us. Unavailable
to use. Our rapacious use. And though
the rocks buzz
with energy, pulsating in tune

with the earth's vibrations, their drone

is beyond what we hear. So
the ground truth is a constant
revision. Who can read
across the vertiginous stanza
breaks? And what

possible explanation is there
for our wrong turning, but our insistent
repetition of the wrong turning?

All that aluminum in the sky around San Francisco.
The heavies taking off, flying east. Or south
with us to Mexico.

Cuánto cuesta ir al centro, señor?

In bushes behind the bar, a whistling frog
tries hopelessly to compete with patio speakers
blasting rancheras.

To die of exhaustion before it can mate?

I pump the empty bathroom towel dispenser
a few more times for its sound—
like a bulldog wheezing.

No pueden ver sus propias vidas, the woman
at the next table says as she makes a square
in the air with her thumbs and index fingers.

A loner on every other stool, staring into his beer.
Around midnight

we stroll past a smattering of young people
gathered on the steps of the closed museum
where a local teenager strums, and they're all
singing "Hotel California." By the time

I wake, you're back
from the market with poblanos and two balls of salt.

In the guide's truck bed, dirty hiking poles
and shin guards, a toolbox
welded from diamond plate and angle iron.

We pass miles of nothing but desert grass
dotted with palmilla. Heat shimmer.

Just before we begin to trek
between the scalloped canyon walls,
he shows us how to rub down our pants
with crushed stink bugs
to protect against snakes.

*

But here, you said, at the time of our intrusion,

you said this zone here is not one of the earth's sentences

but an overdub of stutters, here where we're walking

on this slumbering crack, a complex, you said,

of tensions right here, and you bent and touched

your finger to the warm, ant-fenestrated dirt

while I surveyed the hairpin turn in the arroyo beside us

and then you stood and brought it, your finger,

to my lips, you said here, and you watched me

as the taste, part you part earth, brought a change to my face.

*

When they tell me it's narcissistic
to speak of regrets, to let myself circle
in this whirlpool and to go on
about it, when they tell me I need
to move forward, to focus outward,
to offer my attention to others,

aren't they themselves prompted
by an overbearing concern for control
which is another form of narcissism? Isn't
this very mourning a constancy
to something beyond myself? Don't
I have the right to my own experience
of heartache and anguish and failure?

You do, child. But not for so long.

At peace means despair
has settled in its place.

Oh no. I see suddenly
that what I've caught in my trap
is the favorite hunting dog
of the God of Excoriation.

And everything is scarcely moving
like the mirage of a lake.

No one bears tragedy. It holds you in place.

Indisputable, they say. Two
plus two equals four. As though
reason unlocks truth,
the logic of the universe. But
for some, two plus two
equals many. Which isn't less true.

To reach for a world
that is out of reach.

What seest thou else in the dark backward?

Though no one calls, I look back again.

Which is when. Which is when I see you.

Stripped down, what is there, really,
between us? Is there? There, now.

Bees thrum in your eyes.

When the thumb is tucked to sleep, the fingers open.

The goal was never knowledge, but attentiveness.

Take the horned, green head of this One-
eyed Sphinx caterpillar, for instance.

Or the piston-driven respiration of trees.

Even the shape of my body is a response
to the world's importunity.

And how can I be separated out? Am I ever just this?
Don't I continually outdo myself?

*

Like the magnet beneath a glass table of iron shavings, you orient me.

Your warm, conductive flesh. Your scent
pooling into the hollows above your clavicles.

It was your imperative that launched me forward. After I had stopped.
After the currents of possibility
coursing through my arteries were choked off
with windrows of memory, doubt, and reassessment.

Arm in arm, coming down the stepwell.

I, the revenant, the forgotten unapostle of adoration.

And I'd been forewarned
by the example of those who—
to keep the spectacle of reality
from distracting them—
invented boredom. Now
each moment of their lives
doesn't seem so momentous. While

even your small, daily enthusiasms are emphatic. So
I find the expeditions of your conversation transfixing.

Faithfulness, our commitment to what we don't know.

So vivid in your eyes, the ecstatic commotion of feeling.

And in your buoyancy: the impulse to live.

Even when he's far from her, her voice
remains with him, within him. Sometimes
he hears himself speak to himself. In her voice.

What is it you're thinking, your forehead knotted up like that?
I was thinking of you.
What were you thinking?

We may appear to survive
even after the substance of our lives
gives way like a tent cloth
collapsing with a soft huff.

The core hollows out, but the tree lives on.

So it was until I swan-dived into you and
into you. And you stood up through me.

From Singapore she sends him a photograph
a friend has taken. She's sitting at a small pool
set with coral tiles while an invisible swarm
of goldfish defoliates the balls of her feet.

He spends the night sleepless, failing
to keep from rewinding and replaying her voice message.

As if something not being said was all he could hear.

Around him, the hillsides are laned
with burnt trunks and their shadows.

All the while she travels, he keeps her white
paper napkin where she left it on the TV tray
by the couch. And on it, her chopsticks
stained with fragrant squid ink.

Turning his head toward the kitchen, he notices
and plucks from the shoulder of his sweater
a single long strand of her hair. Holds it up
between thumb and forefinger under the living-
room light. Notices a kind of low
ringing in the air, back behind everything else.
He glances around the empty room—looking for what?
Places the hair back where it had been on his shoulder.

You are the love of my life.
No. You are the love of your life.

Did he keep his word, or only his skepticism?

From the lake's edge, his eyes remain fixed
on an indeterminate wake. What is it
swimming just under the surface?

While the sun trembles in an argentine sky.

Sparkling clots of froghopper foam
cling to purple thistles grown up
through cow paddies along the creek. He walks
for hours with the constant sense that
he's only half-seen something. Vanishing
lizard tails on either side of the forked path.

With darkness and a heavy mist
falling, the way back to the pasture
becomes unrecognizable, completely alien.

In such hazy places, in moments whose meanings are never clear,
he thinks he catches her scent, that wood-spice
of cumin and verbena. Which is when

the truth breaks through to him.

As a black bull steps out from the fog.

*

Glancing up from the page to acknowledge
no one there. Which is only
one of your forms.

Your voice, a rapture of silence. Incessant
immanence.

I look away. I look
back. And all has changed.

Like a moth hitting the windshield.

A lit cigarette tossed from a car
bursting into sparks along the dark road.

I recall the human event
of you turning your face
toward me for the first time. How
many lives before I fail to see it so clearly?

There are times when, in our mind at least,
we must swim back upstream
to where the love originated.

That it might be what it was and is again.
In bed and out.

Because all that is in me is in your eyes.

You, who are the discharge of my singularity.

*

Who says you can't stay fixed on the boat's wake?

While the light lowers itself over the tree line and the stars begin to
    appear in sets.

How is it that the scorched amber glow
of the sun lingers at the horizon as though
it were the last shred of sincere feeling
sloughed from a personality
being extinguished?

We find ourselves approaching the edge of a commitment
whose depth we can't fathom, one that draws us
inward, in pulses, into ourselves, into each other,
into the prismatic intuitions
no blow or grief can erase. As even now
we engender a rhythm of relation
in this extended embrace.

*

The oldest extant pigment of color, scraped
from rocks beneath the desert,
is a flaming pink.

Spring comes. It breaks into me. You
break into me.

While the past goes on lifting out of itself like a wave.

But you had the sense to linger by the shore
as I snorkeled out over the nebulous,
slo-mo, shark-eerie drop off
of the shelf.

*

He's seduced by an intelligence that outleaps his own.

She's funny. Her jokes
become his. And she adopts
certain gestures from him
into her vital movements.

Each is charged by the charge in the other.

Each summoned to what
if not a sacred assimilation.

The moments brim with her liveliness. He's
aching to see all the colors in her spectrum.

And her ass, like two cloves of garlic.

After all they've undertaken and lived through,
have they effaced one another's outer limits?

Everything seems the same. The Pacific
chorus frog in the front yard is answered
by the one in the back. The firebox remains
clammed shut. Don Mee's green birdhouse
hangs from the limb of the olive tree. Only now
it is all quivering. Holding its breath.

When they pass in the morning in the kitchen,
he spins her around and kisses her.

As though in response to the question:
How do *you* answer for *your* existence?

*

I admit: all my gestures are addressed to you. You,
the starting point, the rhapsodic precedent.

Even now, these years later, I'm still
turning my head, listening for your words.
I know I imagine them into being, there
being nothing else I can imagine.

In photographs taken of me before we met
I see only the impending joy in my face.

Audible sunlight, the western meadowlark's opera.
And each dawn, your sing-song greeting to the cat.

As if our happiness had its own desire,
the desire to trill, to cling to us, to stay.

*

She processed experience faster than others. She
was more immediate. It even seemed,
for a while, her feelings could keep pace with her life.

But when the god steps into you,
your shadow disappears.

Still, as long as my eyes stay on you, you stay.

Though I peg one moment as decisive,
I know it is the consequence of a lifetime.

These days, with no alarm,
I keep waking at the same time. As if
iteration might introduce me to some meaning
not limited to resemblance.

Meanwhile, do you hear it? That
insistent knocking outside the house?

Which is when the brachiomandibular muscles contract,
forcing the hyoid bones forward in their sheath
so that the Gila woodpecker's long tongue—
forked at the base of its throat, coiled
around its skull, and anchored to the eye socket—
is propelled through the drill hole
into a gallery of beetles
below the barky skin of a rotting saguaro.

*

They pass the burnt carcass of an Oldsmobile rusting in an expanse
    of sand.

Cyphered quiet at the skirt of Calico Peaks and
turkey buzzards, high up, weightless as flecks of ash.

Surely it is real, this swirl of light.

But what is impossible in this life is impossible in any other.

He finds her leaning over the fence, talking
to the goat. *Sweetheart, who taught you
to stand on your hind legs like that?*

It's her spring voice, fuzzed
by March pollen. The nidorous
odor of his testosterone in the air.

Burned oaks footed in naked rock crevices.
A light so sharp, it's percussive.

Is there an emotion of awareness?

Do they refind their bearings in the genuine
or will elation always be contingent? Snagged

between the slow unfoldure of the self
from its familiarities
and the mesmeric qualities of hope.

*

She wasn't fixed, necessarily, on happiness
which she couldn't, in any case, distinguish
from luck. What she wanted was to flourish.

Happiness, she said once, is for amateurs.

He spoke earnestly, looking into her eyes for confirmation—
of what? She listened as though there could be a secret
wrapped in each of his words. His breath was a little bad.
His eyes, round and small and without
noticeable lashes. Like the eyes of an eel, she thought.

Yes, she answered. In a voice he can
still hear— as low and sure
and fragile as lichens. A sound
like stars in the daytime sky. *Yes,
we'll make it last.*

Which is when a squadron of California
quail burst from the coyote brush.

Because if love doesn't survive, why would you want to?

*

In the city, a weather of zeros-and-ones

cascades through rising static, while here

in this xeric topography, we fold ourselves

into the circumstance of desert foothills

chewed away by leprosies, toothed winds, and

sudden rains. Will you let me

approach you? Bend forward

and touch consequence, tenderness, leave

the trace of my fingertips

on your throat's dimple, your

clavicle, nipple? Lean in. In

my mouth, the sound of

your name has changed.

*

An olivine moon. The sum of what
he knows of her is balanced
on what he doesn't know.

Came home early and caught her
singing in the shower.

His insides stirred as though, for lunch,
he'd eaten sardines and a parrot.

The covenant and affirmation of being
his beloved's beloved.

But the true explanation of an intimacy
is the duration of that intimacy.

Like an evening coming alive
with fireflies, he feels himself
pulsing from vivid amber to green.

The Mojave, where whatever he is
debouches from its sluice. What
is more sacred than the gratuitous
opulence of this emptiness?

She can see how she looks
to him. In his face, can
see she is gorgeous.

How do I measure
the inner experience of aging?

The *and yet*, the *and still*
of your affection.

You disappear into my line of sight.

As *here* takes its shape from you.

*

In long-sleeved shirts and hats with neck flaps,
they hike a thaumaturgic canyon path
limned with tall mustard flowers.

*

Where is the place for them in
geologic time? She lifts binoculars
to her lined face.

*

There, where palms sway over a dry spring,
they come to encounter themselves
penetrated by birdsong, standing among trunks
and vines risen from the ground
like the births and messages they are.

*

Someone has spray-painted two orange arrows
in opposite directions across the road
to let the next earthquake
know which way
to go.

*

Walking the rift, they keep their voices
small. Shallow vibrations
scuttle along the fracture zone.

*

Clusters of ramose fissures reticulate the plain.
Thirty feet from where it was displaced,
that's where the arroyo realigns.

*

A full day's trudge under the sun. And no
turning back. Everywhere
they go, it's as though the land's
smooth body has been subject to the cuts
of an amateur's autopsy. Then,

*

in the hours following a brief rain,
cracks at the edges of long wounds
in the terrain begin ferning.

CODA

RIFT ZONE

And so find myself in a shell
jacket and approach-shoes
strolling past boulders
on the xeric canyon path
limned with mustard flowers
as though it were my garden,
as though I'd never
drawn those distinctions
that separate me out,
as though I hadn't long back
expelled myself from all that

wasn't myself. But where
is the human place
in geologic time? Is there
some quality in me that links *I am*
to the remainder?— to whatever
is left over? Left out. What
in the world
have I left out of me?

Adjusting a headband beneath my hat,
I lift the binoculars
to my lined face. Displaced
by lateral slip, the mountain's
slopes have gone wonky.
A *human* life, what
is that anyway? Even here
at the disturbance zone, I find

myself pierced by birdsong,
standing among trunks and vines
risen from the ground
like the births and messages
they are. A riven land, this

place belongs solely
to itself. From the wall
of a crevasse,
tree roots jut out
into air. The fault is the earth's
junction box,
where its wires are
bared. The conflict churns
under ground howling out
in the faintest of decibels. Of course

there were signs, but no
one of us witnessed the ballet
of trees as the tectonic
strain below them rose
and they inclined suddenly
toward each other
from where they stood rooted
to the parted lips of a widening
rift. The earth humphed and
rolled and the trees bowed forward
and held their new pose
which strangely resembles a gesture

of devotion. But back at the start,
I was occupied

with myself as though I were
never to be a part. As if
I weren't both *in* and *of* it. Of
what? So I hike the long
fault for some new
point of view, asking, muddled
with anxiety, what comes next. Now
that I can't claw my way any further
from what doesn't resemble me. The earth
keeps stretching, knuckling, stretching
out from under itself, hungry
for a new shape, a new address. It has
tossed itself loose from its sheets and risen,
leaving behind a note
I suppose I could read if I tried. The fissures

run through everything, even through
my remaining years — which I can count, probably,
on my fingers. I fan them out and stare
at their ruptured, upturned faces, the faces
of my remaining years. I try
re-shuffling them, but no. They grimace
one through the other, they release
a sulfur smell; their solidity dissolves like long clouds
of filth entering a river. My time is here and
not. Feet dangling, I'm perched
at the edge of what? listening to the crackle,
the extinctions of small breaths
around me. While crevices bloom from the crevices,
and dust lifts and catches in dry caches of wind.

Heat and silence. Still, the ground insists
its openings will be filled. Why
not apply? Apply myself. Over and over. This argument

goes beyond me. I who have never been
homeless. Groundless. Am I just going
to stand gobsmacked
at the mirror while my years run out? What

is left of experience that hasn't
been measured? Is there
an app for that? As I bend, I feel
the weight of the specimen stones
I carry in my jacket pocket slide forward.
As I continue my solo descent
along the canyon's seam. As I sip
and hold a quick breath. As I slip from sight
into a chimney of rock.

ACKNOWLEDGMENTS

The short poems "In long-sleeved shirts," "Where is the place for them," "There, where palms sway," "Someone has spray-painted," "Walking the rift," "Clusters of ramose fissures," "A full day's trudge," and "in the hours following" were included in the Ashwini Bhat and Forrest Gander exhibition *In Your Arms I'm Radiant* at Shoshana Wayne Gallery, Los Angeles, January–February 2023.

"But here, you said" appeared in the *New Yorker*, October 2, 2023, Kevin Young, ed.

"Summer roadrunners," "But I was a jukebox," and "Now he's watching scarves" appeared in *Harper's Magazine*, July 2023, Ben Lerner, ed.

"Searching for their night roost" appeared in the *Atlantic*, July 2023, Walt Hunter, ed.

"Men arm themselves with facts," "Back here, he imagines her," and "Back at Lana's Diner" appeared in *Revel*, Summer 2023, Atsuro Riley, ed.

"But how do you tell," "Shifting light animates the room," and "Oh no" appeared in *Lana Turner: A Journal of Poetry and Opinion*, Fall 2023, Calvin Bedient, ed.

"Wiper blades splashing me," "But doesn't thinking happen," "All this theorizing about the erotic," "Even when he's far from her," and "The coffee capsule" appeared in *Action, Spectacle*, Summer 2024, Adam Day, ed.

"Not, you say, to fall back," "Before we knew of our friend's death," "When they tell me it's narcissistic," and "Like a towering wall" appeared in *Jung Journal: Culture and Psyche*, Summer 2024, Paul Watsky, ed.

"So what if worlds are boundless" and "Now the Joshua trees are withering" appeared in the *Overland Review*, vol. 1, Fall 2024, Eden Nobile, ed.

"She wasn't fixed" appeared in the *Nation*, Kaveh Akbar, ed.

"The oldest extant pigment of color," and "The Mojave, where whatever he is" appeared in *Ex-Puritan*, Puneet Dutt, ed.

"Now there are creases" appeared in the *New York Review of Books*, Jana Prikryl, ed.

"Orange lichen," "Because the tree line," "I pour arnica," "All that aluminum," "Glancing up from the page," "He's seduced by an intelligence," "They pass the burnt carcass," and "An olivine moon" appeared in *Poetry Review*, Wayne Holloway-Smith, ed.

Thank you Ashwini Bhat, Jack Shear, Katie Peterson, Don Mee Choi, Monica de la Torre, Dan Beachy-Quick, Brenda Hillman, Bob Hass, Raúl Zurita and Paulina Wendt, Dong Li, Julia Fiedorczuk, Rosmarie Waldrop, Roberto Tejada, Calvin Bedient, Declan Spring, Jorie Graham, Peter Sacks, Lynn Keller, Arvind Krishna Mehrotra, Katherine Hedeen and Victor Rodríguez Nuñez, Ben Lerner, Joyelle McSweeney, and Sasha Dugdale.